Church Membership Matters

Mark Agan

CONTENTS

INTRODUCTION

In most congregations, there are varying degrees of commitment among the members:

The Faithful Few – *they can be counted on to do whatever is needed in the church.*

The Fairly Faithful – *they attend somewhat regularly but they are not as dependable.*

The CEO's – *they attend only on **C**hristmas, **E**aster, and **O**ther special days.*

The FPO's – *they use the church for **F**uneral **P**urposes **O**nly!*

So, is church membership really important? Can a person still be a good Christian and NOT be a member of a church? These are some good questions that we need to consider.

When a person is born again, they are automatically added into the family of God, but the Bible clearly teaches that every believer is also to be a part of a local New Testament church.

So, let us take a few moments to look into God's Word and see why *Church Membership Matters.*

CHAPTER 1

Here's the Church; Here's the Steeple

I remember being taught as a child how to clasp my hands together and make a church. My fingers would be interlocked together and then I was told to say, "Here's the church; here's the steeple. Open it up and here's the people."

Growing up in a preacher's home, church has always been a familiar place to me. My grandfather was a pastor and my father was a pastor so church has always been like a second home for me. But not everyone is as familiar with church and all that goes on there.

Just mention the word church, and different thoughts will come to the minds of different people. Some people view the church as just another civic club or community organization. They see it as something that every good, moral, upstanding person should be a member of because it is "the thing to do." Others attend church more out of convenience than out of conviction.

To get an accurate definition of a church, we must see how God defines the church. As we look into God's Word, we will see that it takes more than just a building with a steeple to make up a church. Church is more than hymn books, offering plates, and Sunday School Classes.

Likewise, there are certain prerequisites when it comes to becoming a member of a local New Testament church.

> *Acts 2:46-47 And they, continuing daily with one accord in the temple, and breaking bread from house to house, did eat their meat with gladness and singleness of heart,*
> *47 Praising God, and having favour with all the people. And the Lord added to the **church** daily such as should be saved.*

2

What Is A Church?

The word *"church"* comes from the Greek word *ekklesia* which means "a called out assembly." So, by definition, the church is a body of baptized believers who have been called to come out of the world and assemble together. In its simplest terms, the church is basically a family gathering of believers.

In Matthew 16:18, Jesus distinguished the church from other assemblies of the day with the personal pronoun "MY" when He said, *"I will build **my** church..."* Therefore, a New Testament church is the "Lord's Assembly."

There are three important facts to keep in mind concerning an "assembly."

1. An assembly must be LOCAL.

Some people believe in a universal church. They say the church is simply a universal organization made up of people from all around the world who are believers. But according to the Bible, the church is an assembly of believers who have **come together**. People cannot come together and yet be all over the world. For example: an automobile is an "assembly" of many different parts but it would be crazy to think of it as being everywhere. We do not call it a "universal car!"

In all but about 15 instances, where it is used in a generic sense, the word "church" or "churches" is always used in connection with definite, geographical locations.

2. An assembly must be VISIBLE.

Some people also believe this universal church is invisible. But people cannot come together and not be seen. I think one reason people like the "invisible church" theory is because it allows them to move around from church to church without having to be committed to any one church in particular. I think they also like the thought of an "invisible church" because then they can give "invisible tithes!" Yet when you study churches in the Bible, you find that all the churches mentioned in the New Testament were local, visible churches.

> **Acts 15:4** *And when they were come <u>to Jerusalem</u>, they were received of <u>the church</u>, and of the apostles and elders, and they declared all things that God had done with them.*

When Paul wrote to the churches at Philippi and Thessalonica, he wrote that he desired to come and see them.

4

1 Thessalonians 2:18 Wherefore we would
have <u>come unto you</u>, even I Paul, once and
again; but Satan hindered us.

He couldn't have planned to go visit them if they
were not a local, visible church.

3. An assembly must be ORGANIZED.

The word "assembly" implies organization. There
is no organization to a universal, invisible church, but
a church is an organized assembly. It is not a disorderly
mob.

In 1 Timothy 3:15 the church is likened figuratively
to a house. The house you live in was assembled. Does
a pile of wood, bricks, and mortar constitute a house?
Of course not. They must be assembled according to a
plan or blueprint. Just like a cup of sugar, a couple of
eggs, and some flour individually does not constitute a
cake. They must be assembled according to a recipe.

The church should also be made out of the right
components. You wouldn't build a car out of paper,
water and meat! You wouldn't make a hamburger out
of sawdust and dirt. Likewise, a New Testament church
is not to be made up of just anything or anyone! The
Bible is very specific in exactly *what* a New Testament
church should be made of, and exactly *who* can be a
member of it.

5

Who Can Join The Church?

In Acts 2:41, the Bible gives us the qualifications for a person to become a member of a local New Testament church.

Acts 2:41 Then they that gladly received his word were baptized: and the same day there were added unto them about three thousand souls.

According to the Bible, **the first priority of church membership is SALVATION.** Notice it says, *"Then they that gladly received his word..."* Only those who heard the Word and had received the Word were qualified to join the church.

Don't misunderstand me, anyone is welcomed to attend the church. It makes no difference if they are religious or not. It doesn't matter if they are good, moral people or if they are the biggest sinner in town. Everyone is welcomed to attend church, but according to the Bible, only those who have made a profession of faith in Jesus as their Savior can become a member.

So, how does a person trust Christ as their personal Savior? That is a very good question. In fact, it is such an important question, that the answer to it will determine your eternal destiny!

6

Many believe they can get to Heaven through any religion or by doing good works, as long as they are sincere. The problem is, one day they will stand before God at the Judgment and find out they were sincerely wrong!

The Bible is very clear on the matter. There are not many different ways to Heaven; only one. To understand what the Bible says about salvation, there are several truths you must understand.

1. Realize That You Are A Sinner.

Romans 3:23 says, *"For all have sinned, and come short of the glory of God."* Compared to other sinners, we might not look so bad, but God does not compare us to other sinners, He compares us to Himself. And compared to Him, the best person in the world is in trouble!

It is not just because of what we do, but because of who we are. Our hearts are sinful.

Romans 5:12 *Wherefore, as by one man sin entered into the world, and death by sin; and so death passed upon all men, for that all have sinned:*

Ecclesiastes 7:20 *...there is not a just man upon earth, that doeth good, and sinneth not.*

7

The Bible says that because we are sinners, we have broken God's law and we will have to stand before Him on Judgment Day to give account of ourselves.

Romans 14:12 *So then every one of us shall give account of himself to God.*

Hebrews 9:27 *And as it is appointed unto men once to die, but after this the judgment:*

2. Realize There Is A Penalty for Sin.

Romans 6:23 says, *"The wages of sin is death..."* We get our wages on payday, but the Bible says sin also has a payday; it must be paid for.

The mistake many make is they think they can pay for their sins by being a good person, by getting baptized or by joining the church. But the Bible doesn't say, "The wages of sin is being a good person" or "The wages of sin is baptism" or "The wages of sin is church membership." Notice it says, "The wages of sin is **death**." According to the Bible, the only way I can pay for my sin, and the only way you can pay for your sin is to die and spend eternity in Hell.

Now that's not very good news, is it? So, let me tell you the good news. The good news is that we cannot earn eternal life because it is a *free* gift.

8

Romans 6:23 *For the wages of sin is death; but the gift of God is eternal life through Jesus Christ our Lord.*

A gift is always free. When your boss hands you your paycheck on payday, you don't say to them, "Thank you so much. You are so kind to give this to me. How can I ever repay you?" No, because you earned it. If you work to earn something, then it is no longer a gift, is it? On the other hand, imagine your parents handing you a nicely wrapped gift at Christmas time and after you open it they say to you, "That will be $19.99 please." If you have to pay for it, then it never was really a gift to begin with.

3. Jesus Died To Pay Your Penalty.

The Bible says in Romans 5:8 that God demonstrated *"..His love toward us in that while we were yet sinners, Christ died for us."*

Jesus did not wait for us to become a better person. He did not say, "If you will clean your life up and become the best person you can be, THEN I will come and die on the cross for your sin and save you." NO! He came *"while we were yet sinners."*

So, if the wages of sin is death, and Jesus died for us, then He paid the wages of sin, didn't He? Therefore it is a free gift.

9

4. We Must Receive God's Gift of Eternal Life.

The fourth thing we must do is we must respond to what Christ did on the cross for us. We must receive His payment for our sin.

Romans 10:9 *That if thou shalt confess with thy mouth the Lord Jesus, and shalt believe in thine heart that God hath raised him from the dead, thou shalt be saved.*

We receive God's gift of eternal life by simply confessing with our **mouth** what we believe in our **heart**. The Bible says our heart and our mouth must agree. Why? Because we can say things with our mouth that we do not believe in our heart. Just *saying* you believe in Jesus does not mean you truly do in your heart.

Romans 10:13 *For whosoever shall call upon the name of the Lord shall be saved.*

Salvation is as simple as believing that Jesus died, was buried, and rose again to pay for your sin, and then putting your faith in Him as your Savior.

If you truly believe that, then by faith call upon the Lord right now. Tell Him that you realize you are a sinner in need of a Savior and you want His

10

forgiveness. Tell Him that you will trust Him and Him alone to take you to Heaven when you die.

The second priority of church membership is BAPTISM. Acts 2:41 says, *"Then they that gladly received his word <u>were baptized</u>..."*

Baptism is NOT salvation, but it IS the first step of obedience for a new Christian.

If you *"gladly received His word"* then you will want to identify with Christ and baptism is the first way to do that. Baptism is simply an outward expression of what has taken place on the inside. It symbolizes the death, burial, and resurrection of Christ.

So, baptism is about identification not salvation. Therefore, baptism only comes after salvation, never before. Why? Because, before salvation, baptism doesn't symbolize anything. Just like a wedding ring doesn't symbolize anything until AFTER you are married, a person getting baptized first is trying to symbolize a commitment they have not yet made.

The third priority of church membership is JOINING. The next part of the verse says, *"and the same day were <u>added</u> unto them..."*

Even the Apostle Paul felt it was important to join the church. Acts 9:26 says, *"And when Saul was come to Jerusalem, he assayed to <u>join</u> himself to the disciples:"*

11

I asked the question earlier: "Can a person be a good Christian and NOT be a member of a church?" I believe the answer is "No."

Now, I did not say a person could not BE a Christian and not be a church member. I am saying that according to the Bible, they cannot be an OBEDIENT Christian and not be a part of a local New Testament church.

There are only two positions a Christian should be in: they should either be an active member of a local church OR they should be *seeking* to be an active member of a local church. I do not believe the Bible allows any middle ground.

"But what is the benefit of becoming a member of a church," you ask? That is a good question; one I will answer in the next chapter.

CHAPTER 2

Membership Has Its Privileges

Everything from airlines to American Express lets us know that there are privileges to becoming a member of their club. They each offer their own perks and benefits when you become a member with them. I believe the reason church is not a priority with many is because they have lost sight of the privilege we have to be a member of God's church.

Part of the problem comes because we want to see immediate benefits. For instance, when some start having family problems, they begin going to church thinking their problems will be solved overnight. When their problems are not solved quickly they quit

CHURCH MEMBERSHIP MATTERS

going thinking it was doing no good. It is kind of like a man having a heart attack then going to the hospital and expecting to be better the very next day. Your problems did not happen overnight and therefore will not be solved overnight.

Just as you cannot cultivate a lasting relationship with your spouse in one day, you cannot cultivate a walk with God in only one church service. It amazes me how many people think they can get all they need to face the trials life throws at them by only attending church one hour every other Sunday. That is about like thinking we could get enough nutrition by eating only one meal a week.

The church is a place of great blessing to the life of a believer, but some of the greatest blessings of the church may not be seen until we get to Heaven. So what makes the church so special?

1. Christ DIED for the Church.

Ephesians 5:25 says, *"Husbands, love your wives, even as Christ also loved the church, and gave himself for it;"*

One thing I despise is to see someone burn or stomp on the American flag. That makes my blood boil! One reason it bothers me so much is because of what that flag represents and because to disrespect that flag is to disrespect the many men and women who gave their lives for that flag. So, when people burn the American flag, it is a disgrace to those who died for it. Likewise, when we ignore church, we are showing disrespect to something for which Christ died. We are saying it really isn't worth our time when Christ said, "It was worth MY LIFE!"

2. Christ promised POWER to the Church.

Jesus did not promise to give power to the ball field. He did not promise power for the grocery store or any other place. But He did promise power to the church!

> **Matthew 16:18-19** *And I say also unto thee, That thou art Peter, and upon this rock I will build my church; and the gates of hell shall not prevail against it.*
> **19** *And I will give unto thee the keys of the kingdom of heaven: and whatsoever thou shalt bind on earth shall be bound in heaven: and whatsoever thou shalt loose on earth shall be loosed in heaven.*

Mormonism teaches that the church fell into apostasy and ceased to exist. But Jesus said, *"I will build my church; and the gates of hell shall not prevail against it."* How could the church have ceased to exist when Christ said HE would take care of it? How could Jesus lose control of the church when He said in

15

Matthew 28:18, *"All power is given unto me in heaven and in earth"?* So, the church has power because Jesus, Who is the Head of the church, has ALL power!

3. God uses the church to meet certain needs.

There are certain needs that God intended for the church to meet for us that no other place can.

First, God intended for the church to help with SPIRITUAL needs. Acts 4:23 says, *"And being let go, they went to their <u>own company</u>, and reported all that the chief priests and elders had said unto them."* Church provides a place where we can gather with our *"own company"* for prayer and support.

One of the first places you can get support is from your Sunday School Class. That is where needs are first known and met. Many are lacking that support because they are not part of a Sunday School Class.

The church is also the place of spiritual support because it is where the pastor will preach the Word of God that will minister to your spiritual needs.

Second, God also intended for the church to help with PHYSICAL needs. In Acts chapter six, the first deacons were chosen, not to help every widow in the community, but to help the widows of the church.

***Galatians 6:10** As we have therefore opportunity, let us do good unto all men, especially unto them who are of the household of faith.*

It is not the church's responsibility to be the local welfare office, yet that is how some people view the church. We get calls to the church office almost daily, people asking if the church can pay their power bill, or pay their rent. They will not commit to supporting the church through membership and tithing, but they think the church should support them when they have a need.

Our church tries to help with food when a church member undergoes surgery or has a death in the family, etc. But we cannot feed everybody who has a need. The Bible says we are responsible to take care of God's people first. It says, *"especially unto them who are of the household of faith."*

If you want the church to commit to you, you must first be committed to the church. It is true about church like anything else—you get out of it what you are willing to put into it.

CHAPTER 3

What's the Big Deal?

Maybe you are saying to yourself, "What's the big deal? I mean, what is the purpose of church membership anyway? Can't I just float from church to church without joining a particular congregation?"

The mere provision of local churches in God's Word implies a divine purpose for the local church. Anything with a divine purpose should be important to us. The idea of becoming a Christian but never becoming a part of a local congregation is foreign to the Scriptures. So what exactly is the purpose of the local church?

The church is where we get guidance.

There are so many things in life clamoring for our attention. Between our smartphones and social media, we are bombarded with things every day. Everywhere we look, someone else is saying we should do this or that. If we listen to others, we will easily get misled. Therefore, we need a trustworthy guide.

Without a trustworthy guide, we can easily lose our way and not know which way to go. That is where the church comes in. God gave us the church so we would have a place to go for the right guidance.

There are two specific areas in which the church gives us guidance.

1. It gives guidance through <u>Direction</u>.

The church is able to give us the right direction because that direction comes from God, Himself.

Acts 2:42 And they continued stedfastly in the apostles' doctrine and fellowship, and in breaking of bread, and in prayers.

The Bible says that they continued in *"the apostle's doctrine,"* or teaching. Church is first, and foremost, a place where the Word of God is preached. One of the first things you should look for in a new church home is not the buildings or the music program or the youth

WHAT'S THE BIG DEAL?

activities. The first thing you should look for is to see if it is a place where the Word of God is preached without compromise!

There are so many who have been led away into false doctrine because they have not been grounded in God's Word.

> **Ephesians 4:14** *That we henceforth be no more children, tossed to and fro, and carried about with every wind of doctrine, by the sleight of men, and cunning craftiness, whereby they lie in wait to deceive;*

The best place to learn the right doctrine is at church from God's Word.

2. It gives guidance through <u>Discipline</u>.

In Ephesians 5:26-27, Paul exhorted husbands to love their wives just like Christ loved the church and gave Himself for it *"That he might sanctify and cleanse it with the washing of water by the word, That he might present it to himself a glorious church, not having spot, or wrinkle, or any such thing; but that it should be holy and without blemish."*

Jesus Christ wants a church that is clean and pure; one without spot or wrinkle. One way in which this is accomplished is through Church Discipline. People don't realize that one of the greatest privileges we have in a church is the privilege of Church Discipline. To those who do not understand what Church Discipline really is, they think of it as being something negative. But actually, it is a very positive thing.

Through Church Discipline, God has given the church the resources to solve any problem, if we do it God's way.

> *Matthew 18:15-17 Moreover if thy brother shall trespass against thee, go and tell him his fault between thee and him alone: if he shall hear thee, thou hast gained thy brother.*
> *16 But if he will not hear thee, then take with thee one or two more, that in the mouth of two or three witnesses every word may be established.*
> *17 And if he shall neglect to hear them, tell it unto the church: but if he neglect to hear the church, let him be unto thee as an heathen man and a publican.*

Church Discipline is really just Christian discipline. In its most simplest form, it is when a person has been offended by another believer and they go to that person one on one and resolve it before it grows into a bigger problem. That is God's method for solving problems in the church. That is how the church remains clean and pure.

The church is where we can grow.

Every human being needs nourishment for their body to grow. Just as physical food gives us physical nourishment, spiritual food gives us spiritual nourishment.

1 Peter 2:2 As newborn babes, desire the sincere milk of the word, that ye may grow thereby:

The church provides a place where believers can come and get spiritually nourished by hearing the Word of God preached. It is through a steady diet of God's Word that you will grow into the mature believer God would have you be.

The church is where we are encouraged.

Hebrews 10:25 says that part of the reason we are to assemble together is for the purpose of *"exhorting one another."* One of the greatest sources of encouragement for the believer is the local church.

I am amazed at the number of people who stop going to church when they become discouraged. When they do this, they are actually hurting their chances of overcoming their discouragement because they are avoiding the one place that is designed FOR encouragement!

23

A person who stops attending church when they are discouraged is about as crazy as a sick person who refuses to go to the doctor and get the medicine they know will make them feel better.

The church is where we serve others.

Galatians 5:13 says, *"For, brethren, ye have been called unto liberty; only use not liberty for an occasion to the flesh, but by love <u>serve one another</u>."* In other words, our love for the Lord will cause us to serve one another and church is where we have an opportunity to do just that.

Far too many Christians have lost their heart to serve one another and have become inactive members. It is kind of like the man who asked the local pastor, "How many of your members are active?" The pastor replied, "All of them are active. Some are active for the Lord and some are active for the Devil, but they are all active!"

If you do not attend church regularly, then you cannot fulfill God's command to encourage and serve other believers. Someone said, "*Coming* together is a beginning, *staying* together is progress, *working* together is success."

CHAPTER 4

Church:
Some Assembly Required

Many times when you buy a child's toy, somewhere on the packaging it will read: "Some assembly required." It means the toy will not work in the way it was created to work if it is not assembled properly.

The church is FAR MORE important than a child's toy, so the Bible teaches us in Hebrews, chapter 10, that for the church to work properly in our lives and give us the most help—some assembly is required. Notice the Bible talks about our closeness, our commitment, and our consideration.

Our Closeness

Verse 22 says, *"Let us draw near..."* In other words, it is OUR responsibility. If we are not faithful to church, it is no one's fault but ours.

First, we are to draw near to GOD. James 4:8 says, *"Draw nigh to God, and he will draw nigh to you..."* The truth is we are as close to God as we want to be and we are also as faithful to church as we choose to be!

Second, we are to draw near to EACH OTHER. Proverbs 18:24 says, *"A man that hath friends must shew himself friendly..."* The best way to MAKE a friend is to BE a friend.

Some people complain because they don't feel connected at church, when the truth is, it is hard to connect with others when you DISCONNECT yourself. If you wait until everyone else tries to connect with you, you may never get connected. It is your responsibility to *"draw near"* to others.

Our Commitment

Verse 23 says, *"Let us hold fast the profession of our faith"* Only one person can keep you from being committed to the Lord—YOU!

Sadly, we live in a day where people are committed to everything but the Lord.

Our Consideration

Verse 24 says, *"And let us consider one another to provoke unto love and to good works."* He is saying that when we choose to miss church, we are not considering others.

Many go to church saying to themselves, "What am I going to get out of this." But church isn't just about us. It is about us ministering to others.

Warning: Danger Ahead!

If I saw a sign that read, "Warning: Danger Ahead!" It would stop me in my tracks! Warning signs are posted for a reason. Warning signs are posted to warn of electrical hazards, or to warn of a dog that will bite. Whatever the reason, a warning sign is meant to make a person pause and consider before moving forward into a potentially dangerous situation.

The Bible also gives us a warning about some potential dangers of which we as believers should beware.

1. The Danger of Fading Affections

Matthew 24:12 says, *"And because iniquity shall abound, the <u>love</u> of many <u>shall wax cold</u>."* I am so thankful we have a church where people still have a love for God; a love to pick up children on our church bus, and a love to support both home and foreign missionaries that go throughout the world to spread the gospel.

But the danger we should beware of is that when we let sin abound in our life, our love for God will wax cold. We need to be on guard because the days are not going to get any easier. Paul said in 2 Timothy 3:1, *"This know also, that in the last days perilous times shall come."*

2. The Danger of Falling Away

2 Thessalonians 2:3 *Let no man deceive you by any means: for that day shall not come, except there come a falling away first...*

How many people do you know who were attending church faithfully at one time but now are no longer in church? What happened? They quit assembling together and as a result they fell away. Not that they lost their salvation, the Bible is clear we can never lose eternal life. But they simply fell away from their commitment to the Lord.

Paul said, *"Let no man deceive you by any means."* They thought church was no more important than anything else. They were deceived into thinking they could take it or leave it, but that is not true. It affects us when we ignore God's church.

2 Thessalonians 2:1-2a *Now we beseech you, brethren, by the coming of our Lord Jesus Christ, and by our gathering together unto him,*

2 *That ye be not soon <u>shaken in mind</u>, or be <u>troubled</u>...*

When people get away from God's HOUSE, and His PEOPLE, and His WORD, they will eventually become *"shaken in mind"* and *"troubled"*.

The word *"shaken"* refers to a boat that is tossed by the waves—they are up one minute and down the next. That is why Hebrews 10:23 tells us, *"Let us hold fast the profession of our faith <u>without wavering</u>..."*

He says they will soon fall away from the faith because a shaken mind produces a shaken faith. God designed it so that the church, the preaching, and the fellowship we get at church brings a stability into our life that we desperately need.

We are living in dangerous times. And as the world outside becomes more unstable, that is all the more reason we need the stability church brings.

"But that place is full of hypocrites," you say. That is true. There ARE hypocrites in the church. But there are also hypocrites at Walmart. There are hypocrites at restaurants, and there are even hypocrites at the ball game. In fact, there was a hypocrite among the twelve disciples named Judas. But Jesus never let people use Judas as an excuse for them not to do right.

My question to you would be: "Do you have your eyes on THEM, or are you coming to church with your eyes on HIM (Jesus)?" If you get out of church because someone else does, then you had your eyes on them and not Jesus.

They're Depending On You!

Another reason we are to assemble ourselves is because people depend on us. If you have children, you have dependents. In the church we are ALL dependents; we depend upon one another.

They're Depending Upon Your Encouragement

Hebrews 10:24 says, *"Let us consider one another to provoke unto love..."* Verse 25 says, *"exhorting one another..."* You cannot encourage someone at church if you are not there. It should be the goal of every believer to show others the love of God when they come into the church.

Notice he uses the word *"provoke."* Normally when we think of provoking someone, we think of making them angry. But that is not what is meant here. Your encouragement should "provoke" others to love God and love His church more.

Think about this: How encouraged would someone be if the ONLY encouragement they got was from what YOU gave them at church?

"But what about me," you ask? Sure, there will be times that you will be the one needing encouragement. But don't just be a TAKER, be a GIVER.

Some people only show up at church when they are down and they want everyone to shower them with encouragement and attention. But as soon as they get what THEY need, you don't see them again until they need encouraging. They become selfish because they get what they need but won't stay in church long enough to help encourage someone else.

Jesus did not come for what WE could give HIM. He came for what HE could give US!

They're Depending Upon Your Example

Paul told Timothy in 1 Timothy 4:12, *"Let no man despise thy youth; but be thou an <u>example</u> of the believers, in word, in conversation, in charity, in spirit, in faith, in purity."* What kind of example does your church attendance set for your spouse, children, or unsaved family and friends?

As Christians, we do not have a right to live as we please. Why? Because somebody is depending on us! I want to do my best to be a good example, don't you?

31

I like what Dr. David Gibbs, Jr. said one time. He said, "I want my NEXT lap to be my BEST lap."

It's Coming! Are You Ready?

***Hebrews 10:26-27a** For if we sin wilfully after that we have received the knowledge of the truth, there remaineth no more sacrifice for sins, But a certain fearful looking for of judgment and fiery indignation...*

If anything ought to cause us to be more faithful to God's house, it should be the fact that Judgment Day is coming! We should not only fear the judgment that is to come, but also the judgment we may face now, because of our sin.

Verse 25 just said we are not to forsake the church assembly, so to deliberately not support God's church is to *"sin wilfully after that we have received the knowledge of the truth"*

I believe there are some people who go from one trial to the next, all because God has brought His judgment into their lives and the reason is because they ignore His church.

Someone once said, "When a man who is honestly mistaken hears the truth, he will either QUIT being mistaken or CEASE to be honest."

32

So, we have a choice to make. Are we going to willfully sin by not obeying God's Word or will we start obeying what we know is right?

Jesus said in John 14:15, *"If ye love me, keep my commandments."* Many will tell you that they love Jesus, but according to Jesus they don't because they are unwilling to obey His command to faithfully attend His church—the place He loved so much He gave His life for it!

Now, once we join a good, Bible-preaching church, there is something we must do to help ensure it is a successful church.

"What is it," you ask? That is the subject of the last chapter.

CHAPTER 5

The #1 Ingredient of a Successful Church

If you were asked to define the single most important characteristic of a church, what would you say it should be? What is the one ingredient of a church that without it, a church cannot be successful?

Some might say the preaching is the most important thing while others may say the music is most important. Some want a church that has a large youth department and others want a church with beautiful facilities. But what is really the most important ingredient to having a successful church?

The answer is a small word, but without it no church will ever be successful because the number one ingredient of a successful church is...UNITY!

That's right. You see, if a church is not united together, then it doesn't matter how good the preacher is or how great the choir sings or how many youth activities there are. Without unity, a church will never grow or move forward in victory. Unity is absolutely essential to a church's success.

1. The INTENTION of Unity

The Bible says that the intention or goal of every believer should be *"Endeavoring to keep the **unity** of the Spirit in the bond of peace"* (Eph. 4:3). The Apostle Paul is not talking about a unity that comes through common goals or ideas. He says that what we are to be seeking after is *"the unity of the Spirit."*

Why? Because it is only *"the unity of the Spirit"* that will bring *"the bond of peace."* We need peace in our society, in our home, and of course in our church. That is why the Bible says we should be *"Endeavoring"* which means to make an effort. If we are going to have unity, we must make an effort to do so. There are some I have seen who did not even seem to make an effort to have unity.

A friend of mine said she was in a church one time where a woman told another woman she would pray a curse on her! Now that would certainly put a damper on a church service, wouldn't it? It doesn't sound like that woman was too interested in working at unity in the church.

There must be a spirit of cooperation if a church is going to be united together. So, Paul says that if a church is going to have unity, it will be intentional, not accidental.

"So, how do we go about living a life that promotes unity," you ask? That is a very good question. Paul answers that question in verse 2.

With all lowliness and meekness, with longsuffering, forbearing one another in love;

Obeying this one verse would solve every church split or fight that happens in many business meetings at churches across the country!

First of all, we are to have **"lowliness"** (or humility), which means "without arrogance or pride in one's position." Some have allowed their position of authority in the church to puff them up in pride. But we must remember that we are nothing but a sinner saved by God's grace!

Next, it says we should have **"meekness"** (or gentleness). This pertains to the way we react when someone hurts us. It is the opposite of sudden anger and retaliation out of vengeance.

Then it says we should be *"longsuffering"* which means "patiently bearing the faults of others." It is referring to being patient with others whose personalities may irritate you.

Lastly, it says *"forbearing one another in love."* That means to support each other through trials. Galatians 6:2 says, *"Bear ye one another's burdens, and so fulfill the law of Christ."* Imagine what it would do for that person who irritates you if you were there to help support them through a trial.

2. The PROVISION for Unity

Later on in the chapter, Paul says, *"And he gave some, apostles; and some, prophets; and some, evangelists; and some, pastors and teachers"* (Eph. 4:11).

In other words, God provided a way for the church to have unity. How? He established offices in the church then fills them with qualified men. Jesus takes certain men who have been given certain gifts, and He gives them to the church. So, God's provision for unity in the church comes through the leaders God sends.

Therefore, when God's people follow God's man, who is following God, there will be unity. Paul said, *"Be ye followers of me, even as I also am of Christ"* (1 Cor. 11:1).

38

God is a God of order. He has a divine order for everything and when that order is respected, unity results. When there is no leader there is chaos and chaos never produces unity. So when God's way is obeyed, then He will work through the *followers* as much as through the *leaders*. That was what the Apostle Paul meant when he said, *"And there are diversities of operations, but it is the same God which worketh all in all"* (1 Cor. 12:6).

Everyone has their place and when we are in our place God can work through us all. We may be diverse in our different gifts and abilities but if our goal is to glorify the Lord we will be united together. That is where unity comes from—knowing that we all have a part in God's plan.

3. The PERFECTION of Unity

Next, Paul says, *"And he gave some, apostles; and some, prophets; and some, evangelists; and some, pastors and teachers;* ¹² *For the perfecting of the saints..."*

He is *not* talking about sinless perfection. We will not be sinless until we are in our glorified bodies. He is talking about maturing the believers. One of the biggest hindrances to Christianity is immature believers.

Jesus Christ gave the church a pastor in order to help mature and grow the believers. The more believers are maturing and growing in the Lord, the more it will produce a spirit of unity in the church. In other words, when you see a church with division, you can be sure they are not mature Christians. Likewise, when you see a person causing division, you can be sure they are not spiritually mature.

Spiritually mature Christians, filled with the Holy Ghost, will be of one heart.

> **Acts 4:31-32** *And when they had prayed, the place was shaken where they were assembled together; and they were all filled with the Holy Ghost, and they spake the word of God with boldness.*
>
> **32** *And the multitude of them that believed were of **one heart** and of one soul: neither said any of them that ought of the things which he possessed was his own; but they had all things common.*

E.C. Haskell said, "When God's people have 'one heart' it doesn't mean they agree on every detail of every decision. It means they all have one goal, and that goal is to glorify the Lord Jesus."

The purpose of the pastor and church is to help grow believers in maturity. So when a person has their own agenda in a church, that is evidence they need to mature.

Proverbs 13:10 says, *"Only by pride cometh contention..."* So when a person becomes contentious, it is because there is pride in their heart. They are more concerned about being *right* than being *obedient*.

4. The OCCUPATION of Unity

The next thing Paul says is, *"For the perfecting of the saints, for the work of the ministry..."* (Eph. 4:12b). The word *"work"* in this verse means 'occupation.' Paul is saying that another purpose of Christ giving the church a pastor is to prepare them to do the **work** (or occupation) of the ministry.

Here is where many churches get off track. They feel it is the *pastor's* job to do ministry, not theirs. But if a church only accomplishes what the pastor alone can do, it will never grow. Not everyone is called to preach or called to pastor, but every believer is called to minister.

> **1 Peter 4:10** *As every man hath received the gift, even so minister the same one to another, as good stewards of the manifold grace of God.*

If you have been saved, then you are as much a minister as the pastor or evangelist is. The Bible says that each believer is to *"minister...one to another."*

A mature pastor is a *ministering* pastor. A mature deacon is a *ministering* deacon. A mature church member is a *ministering* church member. The problem in the average church is they view ministry as something **someone else** does, not something **they** are supposed to do.

Now, it is true that the Lord does not gift everyone with the ability to speak or preach, but the purpose of the pastor is not to just get up and give a little motivational speech. It is the purpose of the pastor to use his gift to prepare the believers to do the work of the ministry.

Think about this. A football coach is not expected to get out on the field and play every position himself. It is his job to oversee the entire team and prepare each player to play his specific position in a way that will help the entire team win the game.

Likewise, no one pastor has been given every gift. Why? Because God doesn't expect the pastor to do it all by himself. He is to teach and train the others to use their God-given gifts in a way that will glorify God and edify the church.

Not everyone is gifted the same or has the same opportunities. That is what Paul was speaking of when he wrote...

Romans 12:4-8 For as we have many members in one body, and <u>all members have not the same office</u>:

5 So we, being many, are one body in Christ, and every one members one of another.

6 Having then <u>gifts differing</u> according to the grace that is given to us, whether prophecy, let us prophesy according to the proportion of faith;

7 Or ministry, let us wait on our ministering: or he that teacheth, on teaching;

8 Or he that exhorteth, on exhortation: he that giveth, let him do it with simplicity; he that ruleth, with diligence; he that sheweth mercy, with cheerfulness.

Paul also wrote in 1 Corinthians about the fact that the body of Christ is made up of many different members.

1 Corinthians 12:12-14 For as the body is one, and hath many members, and all the members of that one body, being many, are one body: so also is Christ.

13 For by one Spirit are we all baptized into one body, whether we be Jews or Gentiles, whether we be bond or free; and have been all made to drink into one Spirit.

14 For the body is not one member, but many.

43

Therefore, as we each assume our own
responsibility for the gifts God has given us, there will
be a spirit of unity that will result.

5. The EDIFICATION of Unity

Next it says, *"For the perfecting of the saints, for
the work of the ministry, for the edifying of the body
of Christ:"* (Eph. 4:12c).

The word *"edifying"* means 'to build up.' So the
next purpose for which God uses the pastor to bring
about unity in the church is for the *"edifying"* or
building up of *"the body of Christ."*

The body of Christ is edified when JESUS is
edified! The whole purpose of unity is so that Jesus will
get the glory He deserves because He is the head of the
church and deserves first place in it.

> ***Ephesians 5:23*** *For the husband is the head
> of the wife, even as Christ is the head of the
> church: and he is the saviour of the body.*

> ***Colossians 1:18*** *And he is the head of the
> body, the church: who is the beginning, the
> firstborn from the dead; that in all things he
> might have the preeminence.*

When the body of Christ is edified, the believers
will begin growing. A lot of church problems could be

44

avoided if some people would just grow up! So as the believers **grow** up, the church is **built** up. So how do we edify one another?

We edify through our Consideration

We are not to live our lives in a vacuum. We are to live our lives with others in mind.

1Peter 1:22 Seeing ye have purified your souls in obeying the truth through the Spirit unto unfeigned love of the brethren, see that ye <u>love one another</u> with a pure heart fervently:

Philippians 2:3 Let nothing be done through strife or vainglory; but in lowliness of mind <u>let each esteem other better than themselves</u>.

The Apostle Paul goes on to say in verse seven that Jesus *"took upon him the form of a servant."* The more like Christ we become, the more of a servant's heart we will have.

In fact, the writer of the book of Hebrews put it this way:

Hebrews 10:24 And <u>let us consider one another</u> to provoke unto love and to good works:

Many people think church is all about them. They say, "What can you offer me?" or "What am I going to get out of it?" But we are not to be selfish; we are to consider others and how we can edify them. That is why church attendance is so important—you cannot edify someone at church if you are not there!

We edify through our Communication

> ***Ephesians 4:29*** *Let no corrupt com-munication proceed out of your mouth, but that which is good to the use of edifying, that it may minister grace unto the hearers.*

Anything we say to others that does not edify is nothing but corrupt communication. When we are hateful, angry, or critical of others, we are not building them up; we are tearing them down. We should speak to others in a way that encourages them in the Lord.

Finally, in Ephesians 4, this great chapter on unity among believers, we see..

6. The DURATION of Unity

> ***Ephesians 4:13*** *Till we all come in the unity of the faith, and of the knowledge of the Son of God, unto a perfect man, unto the measure of the stature of the fulness of Christ:*

46

All of this instruction on unity is not only to prepare us for life on **earth**, but it also prepares us for life in **heaven**! Heaven will be a place of total and complete unity. There will be no factions or cliques in heaven. There will only be one great big family of God living together in unity and harmony throughout eternity!

But until then, Paul said we are to be *"Endeavouring to keep the unity of the Spirit in the bond of peace."*

The local church is a precious gift that we have been given.

If you are not currently a member of a local New Testament church, I want to encourage you to begin praying about where God would have you join and then become an active member and support the pastor and ministries of that church. Why? Because *Church Membership Matters!*

ABOUT THE AUTHOR

If you would like to purchase other books by Mark Agan, you can read more about them on Amazon.com or on his web site at www.MarkAgan.com.

OTHER BOOKS BY MARK AGAN

The Five Most Disturbing Things About Hell

A Home Built God's Way

RESTORATION: There's Life After the Locust

911: What's Your Emergency?

What Are You Thinking? Winning the Battle of Your Mind

Keeping It All Together When It's All Falling Apart

Preparing Little Children for Big Church